Thoreau's Lost Journal

Poems

by

Larry Smith

Westron Press
Toledo, Ohio

Acknowledgments:

"Day in Which Henry David Thoreau
Drinks Mountains and Rivers"
WINDSONG, Summer 1993

"Day in Which Henry David Thoreau
Travels Much in Concord"
WINDSONG, Winter 1992

"In Which Henry David Thoreau
Calculates the Value of Labor"
SEASONS OF THE SANDUSKY, Spring 1995

From *TRIBUTARIES: A JOURNAL OF NATURE WRITING*
Spring 1998 (three poems):

"In Which Henry David Thoreau
Floats on a Rock"

"In Which Henry David Thoreau
Walks into a Field of Light"

"In Which Henry David Thoreau
Contemplates the Way of Water"

This journal of poems is an imaginative work based on years of reading Thoreau, particularly his journals, correspondence, *A Week on the Concord and Merrimack Rivers*, and of course *Walden*. I am also indebted to the body of Thoreau criticism and the biographies of Walter Harding, Robert D. Richardson Jr., and Harmon Smith

Contents:

Henry David Thoreau's Thoughts
on Journal Writing

"Let the daily tide leave some deposit on these pages, as it leaves sand and shells on the shore. So much increase of *terra firma*. This may be a calendar of the ebbs and flows of the soul; and on these sheets as a beach, the waves may cast up pearls and seaweed."

(July 6, 1840)

"My journal is that of me which would else spill over and run to waste, gleanings from the field which in action I reap. I must not live for it, but in it for the gods. They are my correspondents, to whom daily I send off this sheet postpaid. I am clerk in their counting-room, and at evening transfer the account from day-book to ledger. It is as a leaf which hangs over my head in the path. I bend the twig and write my prayers on it, then letting go, the bough springs up and shows the scrawl to heaven. . . . .The crow, the goose, the eagle carry my quill, and the wind blows the leaves as far as I go. Or, if my imagination does not soar, but gropes in the slime and mud, then I write with a reed."

(Feb. 8, 1841)

Myths are made for the imagination
to put life into them.

-Albert Camus

IN WHICH HENRY DAVID DECLARES HIMSELF

I speak of Henry David
as one I am and watch.
As violinist must feel the music
through his own fingers,
as actor must make himself his art,
so the poet must sense his moods
study himself as cat a mouse.
Subject and object, matter and manner
all swallowed up in one.
I lick the salt of sweat
from my own blistered palm,
speak first and last of what I am.

IN WHICH NECESSITY FIRST ENTERS
THE LIFE OF HENRY DAVID

"It's easy," she said, turning away to the stove,
"So easy, you'll forget who you are, doing it."
The wind was banging branches at the windows
while the real darkness of night came on.
"I'd do it myself," she sighed, "Only..."
and she pointed to her large swollen belly.

I grabbed the axe and went out the door.
Grandfather stood on the porch smelling the night wind.
"It's a hard thing you've started to do,"
and his hand took hold of my arm,
"Hard thing to kill anything that's breathing life,
even in the dark." And he let my arm go.

My footsteps led across the snow in some
strange pattern or design, a chain of steps
going slowly. And I thought to myself,
"It will only be as hard or easy as I make it."
The cold wind burned in my lungs like a first smoke,
then blew a light on in my brain.

The animal eyes in the shed,
the silence of straw all around,
the breath of the axe pulling back
the sharp exhale coming down.
I could not count the blood that ran on the ground
that cold New England night.

IN WHICH MRS. THOREAU TALKS OF DIRT AND SMOKE; HENRY DAVID OF FLOWERS AND WATER

Today mother scolded me
for sleeping in the woods.
"Henry, just look at the dirt
around the door. Smell the smoke
inside your clothes. You can't bring
the woods into the house."

I smiled and picked up my boots
black mud caked on their soles,
set them outside with my coat
on a chair. And for a moment
it seemed that I was sitting there.

Touching her arm at the sink, "But, Mother,"
I asked, "how can I keep the woods out?
The fragrance of flowers clings to my skin.
I dip my hands into the pond
and carry a moon to my lips."

Her eyes were a story of light
as she brushed back my hair.

IN WHICH HENRY DAVID FIRST REMARKS ON
THE WAY THAT GIVING RUBS OFF ON THE HANDS

"Take this," she said, and shut the door,
but I know that she walked away more slowly,
as did I sliding my arms through the soft sleeves
of this wool coat of a dead man.
With each step across the yard it passed
more fully from him to her to me.

Today at table while mother talked,
I watched Sophia pass potatoes to John.
And at that moment of the passing,
as mother spoke of slaves and freedom,
both held the dish as if bound
in some alliance of the giving.

Small thing it was, of course,
a gesture in a nod, and yet
it flavored all our food and drink.
The gift inside the giving
felt first in the arms,
it rests like light upon the hands.

A DAY IN WHICH HENRY DAVID
TRAVELS MUCH IN CONCORD

It's true what they say
that I sat in the kitchen and cried
on the day I set off for Harvard.

It was not pride that struck my heart
but fear like night falling
across the flat boards of my house.

On the stoop all week I brooded–
How much would change forever–
Who must I become?

Then Mother brought a cup of water,
sat beside me, touched my arm,
"Henry, what's wrong?"

My words like an autumn flood,
"I cannot see nor hear beyond this moment.
I know not where my path takes me."

Her smile struck me then and now, "Why, Henry,
you can just buckle on your knapsack
and roam the world for your fortune."

A blackness fell over me
that paralyzed my will.
I could not think to breathe.

I saw myself chase dollars down Wall Street
sell books like fish from door to door
build guns for distant wars.

Sophia found me then leaning on the table
pressing tears into my sleeve.
As sisters sometimes do, she knew.

Her arm upon my shoulder, she spoke,
"Henry, you only go out to return
to us and your home."

Her words wrapped me like a shawl
for as I know myself I know
I survive by keeping close.

Like a squirrel, I nest.
My journey lies around me.
I need ramble no further than my yard.

IN WHICH THE NIGHT OPENS
AND SWALLOWS HENRY DAVID

Tonight I walked out with a woman
whose eyes danced in moonlight
whose pale skin yet warms me
as when she pressed my hand to her soft cheek.
We shared the shadows of trees
listening to the crickets till I
could no longer think to speak...
"Ellen" the birds called softly,
and I could only feel her movement from me
as she walked in silence toward her lighted house.
Though I have often sought the stillness
of no-thought, in her presence
I felt myself swallowed into night.

IN WHICH HENRY DAVID PROPOSES HIMSELF
TO FAIR ELLEN SEWALL

Last summer on the Concord River I rowed sweet Ellen,
only I and she before the sky, her slender features
a perfect profile against the sun. I had waited
long enough for John to advance and retreat,
and so I wrote her this note telling how
"the sun of our love should have risen
as noiselessly as the sun of the sea, and we
sailors have found ourselves steering
between the tropics as if the broad sky
had lasted forever." The words floated up
from the sea in the still clear air
till I folded them into an envelope
with her name written across it. I waited
a day, another, and then came her note
thanking me for our walks and "our little row
along the old river," but no words of love,
no thought of our bond. "Sorry, Henry, dear,
but I must be in Boston to help with Mother.
Till another summer, farewell." I tell you
I folded it against my heart, its arrow
another kind of death. For a time I put away
the journal, took out my surveying tools,
walked the rim of others' lives for pay.
How dare I dream so bright a day
could issue in so dark a night?

IN WHICH HENRY DAVID ENTERS AT NIGHT
CONCORD'S UNITARIAN CHURCH

Had anyone been here, I would have remained outside
where I listen long to the sounds inside the woods.
I tap my pipe against the railing, tuck it deep in pocket,
and enter the dark though open door.
I remind you we have not yet learned
to lock our lives as Bostonians do.

It was here the Alcotts baptized Louisa May.
And, how that minister went on about redemption
while a clear sunlight graced her small and rounded face.
It was the year Emerson resigned from the church
after his darling Ellen, frail as a hummingbird,
took her last breath in his arms.

He returned from Europe, I from Harvard.
Still he paced the garden where I weeded.
I recall his blind gaze and rueful laugh,
"So we have come home to Concord!"
At night we'd eat a vagrant meal out on the porch
vegetables seasoned with his talk.

His wife Lydian keeps him together now
walking with him about town, while I play with the boy.
She has this way of making things come out right
like coming in and finding the bread already risen.

Only, this afternoon as she touched my sleeve, and
I feared the day when Waldo should ask me to leave.

I come here at night while Concordians
gather about their firesides or nestle under quilts.
I feel my life turning inside myself, and yet
I know not what my work is. In truth,
I close my eyes in this old house of God,
and am deep in a dark chapel of woods.

IN WHICH HENRY DAVID
WALKS OUT INTO HIMSELF

And who am I these days
living in the house of a friend
wearing his old clothes as my own?
The Emersons are almost too good
with their books and talk. I melt
into the circle of friends, fear I am
losing my divine individuality.
My only escapes now are the old chores
of pencil making, standing inside the
comfort of my father's silence,
and in these poems of others to which I swim.
I love so much their fine cadenced lines.
Once a good line comes out of my head
nothing can bother me. It is the poet
who most I see as myself. And so
I propose to write the poem of Concord
standing deep inside Walden Woods
where this long sojourning may end
and my life begin.

EVENING IN WHICH HENRY DAVID
SPEAKS A MOUTHFUL TO LYDIAN EMERSON

"Sometimes it takes so little,"
she said touching the rose
to her face, "And yet
we miss it." It was
the first time I'd seen her eyes so,
like a forest sunset in a window.

"Lydian," I said, putting the shovel
inside the barn, "You make the
world an easy place to love."
And there in Emerson's garden
a quiet fell between our eyes.

"Henry, please," she spoke
standing in the doorway of the house,
"Give neither credit nor blame,
for those who count success soon lose it."
"That sounds like Waldo," I heard myself say
like one who throws food back at his host.

She stood and stared a long time
at my face, her tiny hands folded
like pedals of a rose.
"Hear me, Henry, for it's I who speak.
Make hills on high ground,
and ponds on the low, but
don't plant seeds on marble,
or try to skate on water."

Inside the dusk I heard her go
and knew the taste of dirt.

IN WHICH HENRY DAVID
AWAKENS IN A CITY

In May I moved out, not to the woods
but a sojourn to the city, finding my way
through a forest of Manhattan crowds
to the rural home on Staten Island
of Waldo's brother William.
Every other day I try on my urban clothes
and enter the cathedral city
meeting Waldo's friends–Tappan and Channing,
James and Greeley–names I recite
on the ferry, as I do for them my plans
for literary labors. Only Greeley hears me,
brightens his eyes with my written words.
The magazines here lack both value
and compensation. I write little and sell less,
a review, an essay on a winter walk in Concord;
mostly I fill this journal reservoir for another time.
The weeks seem to pass quicker than the days.
And so I tutor these dull boys, write in my room
till I fall asleep at dusk, fighting this dumb narcolepsy–
a family curse–so that I find wakefulness a cardinal virtue.
To see each day beneath the eyelids of time
the bright work I can do, and not the iron veil
of what I cannot. Sunrise and sunset
I worship Orion, look to the sea at dawn
and at dusk toward my fair Concord home.

IN WHICH HENRY DAVID UNCLOTHES HIMSELF
IN A MAD SUMMER'S STREAM

I rowed beneath North Bridge
making my way towards Egg Rock
where I paused in summer sun.
My oars held me steady in the current
while I sought my own direction. Should I
drift south with the Sudburry or
work my way northward in the Assabet?
Refusing to decide, I held myself
just at the point of turning till my arms
sung with my straining stubbornness.

Letting myself drift into an inlet, I
heard the wood thrush call through trees.
For what seemed an hour I lay in the bough
as it slid softly among the reeds.
Watching a slow heard of clouds pass by
I swallowed myself entire, complete at last,
nestled on the worn wooden arms.

At the August shank of evening
I unbuttoned myself and over the side
slipped into soft liquidity.
Beside my little boat I stood
watching as the mud settled at my feet.
The evening sun was painting the water
as I lowered my head and drank.

IN WHICH HENRY DAVID RESOLVES
TO DEVOUR HIS LIFE AT WALDEN POND

I am out with it, begun my life
anew in the woods at Walden Pond.
I borrow an axe, another's plot of land,
yet have come to believe all ownership
a kind of lie, an invisibility
before the sun. My friend Channing writes:
"I see nothing for you in the earth
but this field . . . a hut . . . the grand process
of devouring yourself alive." And so,
I've come to baptize myself again
in Walden Pond. I would subsist here
on a field of bush beans, some potato
and corn worked with my own hands.
I fall some white and arrowy pines
for my house frame, face the water,
the railroad far behind. I walk round
its mile and three quarters—
each step a meditation of the here and now.
I would learn each tall pine and oak
as my own face cast across the pond.
These steep banks, these dense vines
and quiet coves—are my home now.
In sheltering myself, I emancipate
my heart and mind, set free the man
I would become. At midnight
on my bunk alone, I gaze out
at the moonlight breathing over
this soft and fertile ground.

IN WHICH HENRY DAVID SURVEYS
THE DEPTH AND BREADTH OF A MAN

I walked and talked with R.W. Emerson
and know none like him anywhere.
He is the poet critic of a nation
and faithful friend to all men and Nature,
whether they know of it or not.
He rises as he lifts all
into a vast and spiritual light
like that which breaks fast through trees.

I find it hard to temper my praise,
yet to give my portrait depth I would admit
the man lacks something of the robust.
One cannot imagine his trundling a wheelbarrow
through the streets of Concord.
His pale hands lack the callous of hard labor
reserved as they are for turning pages
or scribbling higher thoughts.
At times he has disturbed me
by failing to perceive my range
and talked to me as a disturbed child
the more to make his point
yet casting words against the wind.

And though he promised to lend me axe and land
to build my cabin in these woods
he tramps not the forest
from edge of dawn to dusk
to meet me where I am.

It troubles me deeply to think
so fine a mind could be so easily caged.
This acknowledged. I must confess
a sublime love for his true character
which embraces a nation and lifts it
in sweet harmony with Nature.
He makes of it and us
a poetry of the eyes.

IN WHICH HENRY DAVID LAYS PURCHASE
TO THE SHADOWLAND

The evening dark comes in
and fills everything with the
shadows of itself. It's true,
everything we don't think of
is here, along with what we do.
And the sounds are much the same,
ripples over water, full of moonlight,
leaves turning softly overhead.
"I give you back," I think
again and again. "I give you back,"
sing the birds where shadows
reach through me.
To commune with Nature
we need only listen close,
feel for that place where
earth and sky are one.
I lean back in my doorway,
close my eyes and swear
if I didn't know I was here
I could be anywhere.

IN WHICH HENRY DAVID
JOINS THE FLIGHT OF BIRDS

On my pillow bit by bit
I wake to the cry of gulls,
and know I am alive.
As solitary birds love the woods
and deer the tall grass, so I
this dark tea, bitter and strong
as gnarled wood.
                    Yesterday in town
I gathered mother's baked goods,
sat on the porch watching neighbors
stroll home from church.
                        Old Alcott
called me out, "Come over, Henry.
Sit a while," and so we passed
the afternoon under his apple tree,
talking abolition and education.
                          At dusk
I rose, began the long trek back
to my Walden home, wordless
as the flight of birds.

IN WHICH HENRY DAVID WRITES
AS CORN AND GRASS AND COW

Sitting at the edge of this bright meadow,
at the rim of this dark woods,
I sense a man must drench himself
in the moist facts before he ventures
to report a truth. He must *be*
the ripened corn and strong grass
before he paints them, reality
exuding from him as smell
from the muskrat in his ditch.
Nature provides the fact as truth,
so we must reason first with our hands,
let analogies bloom as
sounds from a summer meadow.

The cow beside me sniffs a recognition
takes the fallen apple from my hand,
her rough tongue a long embrace.
A white spot like a daisy on her muzzle,
and on her fawn colored side
I read a map of Asia.
Her bovine presence breathes a fragrance
of cream from all the dairies of the world.

IN WHICH HENRY DAVID WALKS
WITH AN OLD FRIEND

Waldo's voice echoes across the pond
talking as we stroll together here at last
on a path of pine needles and stones.
Two friends once, now forced to compete
in the eyes of men–he the originator,
I the "Emersonian." But this would pass
like the wild geese over our heads
were we not nursing other hurts.
I know he has called me both lazy and cold.
How can he not read my greater ambition
in my acts; how can he not feel my love
for him and fair Lydian?

A true friend is God's gift, is God himself.
Waldo goes off a lecturing down the coast
pressing palms of society, leaving his tribe behind,
while I stay at home pressing sycamore leaves
between the pages of my journal.
The air eats their skin, leaving delicate skeletons,
a living lace to suggest what has been.

IN WHICH HENRY DAVID
BREAKS OPEN AN EGG

Today I count the birds: wild pigeons
in twos and threes, brown thrashers, wild
geese and ducks come in low over water.
Song sparrows and black birds return,
a fish hawk dives through the face of Walden Pond.
The whippoorwill's evening song, a night owl's
deep lament, a startled swan flies up
as my boat chases the moon.
At morning the bright chirp
of a chickadee awakens me
to my early splash in the pond.
It is the Greek sun I feel,
an Aurora of renewal. Let the ministers
clabber among dark pews of redemption.
I seek rebirth in the dawn, the dewy grass,
the day's fresh baptism. An idler
knows best where to play:
among the yellow leaves, in a quick
breeze through a grove of cicada.
All perception of truth is analogy.
Whether we speak it or not,
we reason from our hands to our head.
Water flows and never returns,
so why shouldn't I amuse myself?
A hundred years and someone else
will stroll among these trees, so
why should I not write these poems?

IN WHICH HENRY DAVID
MEASURES THE PAIN

Today I wake in my cabin amidst a summer rain
having passed a fore night and a day in Concord jail.
The cost of resistance is measured only
in my inconvenience, and weighed against
a better health of conscience.
I bore the stares and shaking heads
the constant questioning of motives.
Even Waldo misread my refusal to pay taxes–
True I deplore the Mexican War, the greedy
annexation of Texas, yet it is the abolition
of slavery that drives hardest at the heart.
Resistance to the chains that enslave us all,
to the abuse of another living being,
strikes a blow for human freedom.
As long as any are enslaved, none are truly free–
is the principle; the fact–a man is taken
from his wife, he and his children sold as property,
their bodies used and abused to earn another's wealth.
I lay my hand against the flesh of Marcus Williams
and know my pain is slight, our brotherhood strong.
Though the measure of my resistance stops short
of inflicting pain, I am not unaware of the pain
it does allow. I would bar the door.
I see a day when this all may end in war
if each does not unite his conscience with his life.
I cast my body with my vote that day,
breathe better for the confinement.

31

IN WHICH HENRY DAVID CONTEMPLATES
A FELLOW TRAVELER'S REPOSE

The man Bill Wheeler moved through town
like a wind driving leaves out to fields.
And there I'd find him some mornings
asleep against a tree. His head
a mottled rock upon the grass.
He had neither work nor house nor family to keep,
himself alone without need of good opinion
or news, only the song of some
wood lark to tend to.
Wheeler watched us citizens
as a toad, with choice disinterest.
In the sun he would mend his clothes;
at night, listen to the doves inside the trees.
He had nothing to report or chase down,
and so in silence I admired his good model.

Two months later they found his body
in the brush, so decomposed they had to
pitchfork it into the coffin box.
Some say now he drank himself to death
and died of a cracked heart.
My own mouth tastes both fear and pride
yet would go gladly by his side.
He died the Brahmin's death,
his body fed back into the earth.

IN WHICH HENRY DAVID CONCEIVES
OF UNCOMMON SCHOOLS

At town's center near the cemetery
I surveyed the morning's commerce:
streets swept clean by leaf shadows,
the rumble of wagons over wooden bridges,
those first openings and closings
of cottage doors, and I felt the dull
encroachment of the provincial.

So I rested on the cool stone steps
of our town library until October sun
bade me enter this treasure house
which links us with all towns and men.
Soon I wanted to give books to each citizen
passing, intent on private commerce;
books like candles that might find their place
on each cottage shelf, in each cottager's mind and heart.

Ignoring her failings as I would my father's
I love Concord enough to wish her more.
As noble men and women surround themselves
with the genius of culture and art,
so our noble villages of women and men
become uncommon schools where
we all might learn. Let the wise inhabitants
profess in our streets, together bridge
the darker gulf of ignorance.

IN WHICH HENRY DAVID DRINKS
THE MOUNTAINS AND RIVERS

Already I have slept along rivers
listening to their stories in the night.
Also have I approached and
walked through the face of mountains
where there is no *there*.

Like Lao Tzu
I have lain in tall grass
and given all away.
As cool as autumn,
as warm as spring,
the quiet of seasons rises.

Yet today beside the Concord River
sitting out on a rock
staring down to earth
I feel the sun bake me
till a thought rises:
The mountains are moving, the river is still.

More than my contrariness
this understanding turns inside me
till I lean back to hold the ground
moving with me through time.
And the river's ripple
holds me deep inside.

Across the stream of sky
I glide with red-tailed hawk
winging homeward, moment by moment.

AFTERNOON IN WHICH HENRY DAVID
MEASURES OUT THE MOMENT

Last night I dreamed my father
sitting on the old porch at noon
cutting pencils in the light.
His sure hands were quick on the wood
and yet his eyes were closed.
And I turned and walked away
into the shade inside the trees.

I carried this dream to breakfast
where Mother served questions
with my tea. "Where, Henry,"
she asked across the table oak
as my bread crumbs lay in rows,
"will we get the rent this month?
Can you please, son, think ahead?"
I read the lines around her eyes,
yet turned again to face the woods.

Now, in this deep green I smell
the cool of running rapids
and drink the shadow light of day.
Each vision calls me, robs my air—
a past I know, a future I would not.
I bend and pick the ground apple,
its simple weight the moment's measure;
with open eyes I bite and know
sweet taste of what is now.

DAY IN WHICH HENRY DAVID
CONTEMPLATES THE WAYS OF WATER

Today at the pond before dawn
seated in among the reeds and grass
I watched the day begin. First light
a soft gleam upon the water where I waded
cool and deep and wide till its liquid tongues
bathed my native chest.
My shoulders warmed by sun
I stood there still and
read the clarity of *water:*

To each creeping thing it gives itself continuous.
To each being it extends without preference,
soft and fluid, asking nothing.
Take a stick and strike it. Where's the wound?
Accepting, it cannot be slashed, or cut, or burned.
Yet it penetrates all–wood or stone or metal.
Water's wealth is giving.
Nothing is softer nor more enduring.

I look down at my feet:
three osprey circle overhead.
Ungraspable and clear,
water spreads around me, holds the light.

AFTERNOON IN WHICH HENRY DAVID
GLIDES THROUGH A SHADOW

Driven out of town by a gaggle of girls
gathered about a punch bowl,
women who invite you out yet
in truth never show themselves,
I seek the solace of a road into a woods
and the poetry of leaves in sun and shadow.

In the quiet of an old skiff upon a lake
I follow a current of wind and water
drifting downstream past trees and rocks
in a liquid lapse of thought
that reaches the sublime.
I listen to the voices of wind through pines
and arrive at last upon a shore of calm.

IN WHICH HENRY DAVID WRITES OF HIS WRITING

Six days of labor and the seventh, we read.
Yet each day I find myself writing here
skating pen and thoughts through paper.
As natural as warming sun my writing comes.
I spill myself into these journals
running over with summer gleanings
reaped from fields of walking
yet I know I must not live for but
in them. My life must be
the poem I would write.

The Chinese they say
have the same word for *heart* and *mind,*
and my own heart-mind feeds on words
as well as fish and rice, on deep walks through woods,
finding and making a path. Living is its own explaining.
And though tomorrow these same scribblings
may stare back as empty shells,
I know that a man must live up to his thoughts
wherever they would take him, and if they
lead him back where he began, then the walk alone
will bring him health and home.

5. Set short- and long-term goals with and for your students.

6. Develop teaching styles that are more congruent with the learning style preferences of Black and Hispanic students.

7. Use homework and television to *your* advantage.

8. Communicate so that your real intentions are understood.

9. Establish a climate where children receive the ongoing support and encouragement they need to succeed.

10. Strengthen relations between the home and school.

A brief discussion of each of these tips follows:

1. Develop Strong Bonds with Diverse Students

Any teacher who *really* loves children can motivate children. However, that love must be unconditional. In too many instances, a teacher's love and appreciation of a student is "condition subsequent," that is, the result of certain behavior and abilities in students. Instead, the teacher's love and appreciation should be "condition precedent." Her love would encourage favorable behavior and enhance abilities in students. When a student detects teacher detachment, disinterest, or disrespect, social and personal "bonds" are weakened.

In their research on the causes of delinquency. Fagan and Jones determined that it is the weakening of personal and social bonds with adults that leads to negative peer influences. Schools must provide strong external bonds through efforts to improve achievement, efforts to involve youth in activities perceived as important, and efforts to enhance students' belief in their own abilities and self-determination.[2]

Educators can build student relationships characterized by mutual trust. However, in order to do this, teachers must show a respect for the student and his or her culture, life experiences, and unique learning style. Teachers must see themselves as "learners" as well as teachers. Through a spirit of mutual inquiry, teachers can build bonds with students that foster support and augment achievement motivation.

Once mutual trust is established, the teacher can involve the student in a learning process that takes into account the needs of both student and teacher, as well as the needs of the school (or system) and the needs of society in general. Even when it appears that these needs are in conflict, they are not necessarily at odds.

For example, the student may speak in a non-standard English dialect. The student may be unaware of the *need* for him to be able to speak standard English. The teacher, however—and the school—share a need for that child to be able to speak standard English. Society has a commensurate need for leaders and laborers who are skilled in standard forms of communication. The teacher can help children understand that standard English is required for them to achieve legitimate economic success in this country. At the same time, the teacher should show that the child's previously learned language skills also are valued and have a place in society. In casual conversation students may choose to speak in a dialect, be it Spanish or "Black English." Both are legitimate forms of expression.

The needs of the teacher, the school, the student, and society can all be met through instruction which respects student differences in dialect and culture. An excited, understanding, and caring teacher can bond with a student, regardless of background, language, race, or culture. Further, teachers can show their acceptance of students' speech through the use of poems, stories, and plays that contain dialect. Teachers may occasionally build rhythmic speech patterns and activities into lesson plans and accept slang or cultural dialect while stressing the appropriate and inappropriate uses of such language.

2. Identify and Build on the Strengths of All Students

In many of our schools, too much emphasis is placed on identifying student deficiencies. Once deficiencies are discerned, many educators spend an inordinate amount of time reminding both the student and the parent that those deficiencies exist. If students are allowed to believe that significant adults in their lives, i.e., teachers and parents, see them as incompetent and inferior, many students are likely to see themselves in much the same manner. Their destiny in life often is determined by how they see themselves in their formative years.

All children have non-academic gifts and talents. Every teacher should put two adjectives that describe two of the child's non-academic strengths next to that child's name in the roll book. During the course of the instructional program, children should be provided with opportunities to display their non-academic strengths and talents in ways that enhance academic learning. For example, students can use dramatic or musical skills in role playing or debating.[3]

In teaching parts of speech to Black and Hispanic students in Newark public schools, I discovered quickly the strengths of my dramatic and assertive students. I had my more "dramatic" students perform skits where each person was given a specific role to play. Someone was a noun and someone else was an adjective who had to find the noun he was to describe. Similarly the "adverb" was told to stand next to the noun, rather than the verb; "commas" were told to put themselves in the wrong sequence; "participles" were told to "dangle." The rest of the class had fun specifying where each "part" (person) was supposed to be. My students learned parts of speech through my efforts to teach to *their* strengths.

When a teacher builds on student strengths, it's easier to help that student to clarify his own aspirations for improved behavior and to diagnose the gaps between his aspirations and his present level of performance. The teacher then presents him/herself as a person who appreciates the real worth, feelings, and ideas of that student. The word "teacher" has its roots in the Latin word meaning "to lead or to draw out." Good teachers can bring out the best in every student by acknowledging and strengthening individual and cultural strengths rather than causing self-doubt through a preoccupation with the student's weaknesses.

Family and cultural strengths can be acknowledged through class discussions or writing activities that allow students to relate family and personal experiences that have facilitated their growth, evoked special feelings, or taught them a sense of responsibility. Teachers also can use activities that emphasize those things that make the heritage of a particular student so special, or allow students to engage in dramatic readings or role plays where they have opportunities to dramatize some of the cultural values and behaviors of all races.

In building on the strengths students bring to school, teachers can bring out their hidden potential, thereby strengthening both their social and academic self-images. By building confidence, teachers will be able to abate the fear of failure that causes many Black and Hispanic students to "give up" before their full potential has been realized.

3. Helping Students to Overcome Fear of Failure

All of us have, at some point in our lives, refrained from doing something because we felt we would not succeed. Fear of failure is real. If a child has experienced failure before, he or she does not want to experience it again. A person with a low self-image is likely to use fear of failure as an excuse for giving up or avoiding effort altogether. When individuals have strong self-images, fear of failure can be motivational.

Teachers can help students to overcome fear of failure by first letting every child know that he or she *will* succeed in the learning environment. Teachers must encourage students to see all failure as a learning experience. The feeling of confidence that comes from encouragement will make it easier for failing students to use failure constructively and to persist. Persistence is a learned behavior.[4] Teachers will be hard pressed to teach persistence unless they have it themselves. This means teachers cannot give up on children and must let children know that their support and faith will not evaporate.

Many children who fear academic failure have already overcome fear of failure in social and recreational activities. Teachers can remind children of the experience they had in learning to ride a bike, for example. Although *every* bike rider fell down, children who learned to ride bikes can appreciate the fact that they were able to learn to ride because they *refused* to give up. Similarly, each child can ride the bike called "reading," the bike called "math," the bike called "higher-order thinking," the bike called "science"—but only if he or she *refuses* to give up.

A teacher can help overcome fear of failure in students by informing students of the teacher's intent to involve them in the development of mutually acceptable criteria and methods for measuring progress. By showing students the intention to meet them "where they are," teachers can encourage students to strive for the "3 Ds"—*Determination, Diligence,* and *Discipline.*

Finally, confidence can be enhanced and fear of failure overcome when teachers use activities that build on the non-academic strengths of students and take time to nurture and extol these strengths in the classroom.[5] Students must know that they have opportunities for "legitimate" success through the effective use and channeling of their non-academic strengths. Once they realize they can shoot for specific careers and professional goals that are based on their strengths, children are more likely to be motivated to overcome their academic deficiencies. Table IV presents a listing of some non-academic strengths many Black and Hispanic students are likely to have, and indicates the possible academic or career outlets that can be encouraged as a result of those strengths.

TABLE IV

MATCHING NON-ACADEMIC STRENGTHS WITH CAREER CHOICES

Non-academic strengths or qualities	Possible academic or career outlet
moral responsibility	social service, teaching
compassion	psychology, medicine, nursing
diplomacy	politics
humor and wit	law, writing
sensitivity	counseling, teaching
independence	business, science
courage	civic activism, advocacy organization
altruism	social work, nursing, community organizing, environmental work
manual dexterity	computers, carpentry, graphic arts, locksmith
talent for innovation and improvisation	law, media, engineering, architecture, politics
mechanical achievement	mechanics, plumbing, electrical work, drafting
expressive achievement	performing arts, writing, interior design
culinary achievement	chef, caterer, dietitian
physical prowess	fire fighter, emergency medical technician
social achievement	hotel management, sales

4. Helping Students to Overcome a Rejection of Success

Some Black and Hispanic youth reject "success" as a "White" behavioral norm or as a norm pleasing to the teacher, who in many instances is perceived as "the enemy." These children are then unlikely to put forth very much effort.[6] Teachers can help students overcome this rejection of success by helping them to become more goal oriented.

Success is the progressive realization of a worthwhile goal. Children who reject success generally have not established either short- or long-range goals. Many Black and Hispanic youth fail to set goals because they feel they have minimal control over their fate and will be unable to make a difference in the outcome of a problem, project, experiment, or grade.[7] This belief, common to lower-income students, has been labeled an "external locus of control." Many lower-income youth, as a result of school biases, see no relationship between hard work and success. Additionally, some Black and Hispanic students may have been taught by their parents that rewards very often can be discriminately and inconsistently dispensed.[8] Some Black and Hispanic youth may even fail to set goals because they have little knowledge of what are acceptable goals.

The earlier a child learns the importance of setting goals, the earlier that child will learn the discipline and the necessity for delayed gratification if one is to realize challenging goals. Teachers must understand that Black and Hispanic students, especially, need to believe that goals are attainable and that effort will be rewarded. Educators can instill confidence in students by allowing them to set short-range goals for which they *do* receive support, recognition, and quick reward.

I have already discussed the powerful impact of peer pressure and the "us versus them mentality" likely to develop in some Black and Hispanic students. In a study of low-income Black students at a Washington, D.C., school, peer pressure, and the fear of being accused of abandoning one's social identity, were cited as major reasons why many Black students refused to study, shunned standard English, and avoided what they perceived to be "White" interests (the symphony, opera, and the humanities).[9]

Some students were ambivalent toward academic success because they defined it as a "White perogative" and didn't want to typify White behavior. Spending long hours in study was considered by these youth as emulating Whites. Other students indicated pressure from peers not to excel for fear of being "labelled" homosexual. Many educational institutions have actually contributed to the belief held by some Black and Hispanic students that academic success is "for Whites only" through tracking, ability grouping, and programs which appear to students as discriminatory. Many Black and Hispanic students are made to feel they must "act White" to be successful.

Teachers must help students to understand and appreciate the fact that success is *very definitely* part of the Black and Hispanic experience. Rather than foster the belief that academic achievement is a "White" prerogative, teachers must help Black and Hispanic students to understand and appreciate the standards for excellence set by diverse races and cultures around the world.

If teachers are going to abate the notion among these students that they cannot be successful, that they must choose between their culture and that of the school, teachers also must take steps to eliminate the effects of institutional racism. Black and Hispanic youth are more likely to see academic achievement as a "White" prerogative when there is an over-representation of Blacks and Hispanics in special education classes or lower ability groups. Teachers and administrators must not only eliminate policies and programs that foster such over-representation, they should also:

- Review school policy and revise or eliminate rules that punish students for cultural habits, e.g., wearing African or corn-row hairstyles, signifying or playing the dozens, or being loud or expressive.

- Review instructional materials that belittle, exclude, or stereotype races and cultures. Add materials that are multicultural in all subject areas at all grade levels. If certain biased materials are kept, teachers must know how to use these materials in non-biased ways.

- Develop a basic familiarity with Black and Hispanic culture through staff-development sessions or personal efforts to enhance knowledge. Such efforts might include more reading, visits to art shows or museums, and participating in social events for Black and Hispanic groups.

- Eliminate the word "minorities" from the vocabulary. Schools are preparing students for a *universe* where people of color are not in the "minority" at all.

- Use flexible, heterogeneous, and cooperative groupings rather than ability groupings and tracking.

- Ensure that schools in predominantly Black and Hispanic neighborhoods are financed at least at the same level as schools in predominantly White neighborhoods.

- Incorporate the provision of equal opportunity in the classroom as part of the teacher evaluation process.

Most importantly, teachers must help Black and Hispanic students understand that school success will not require a rejection of their home or family culture.

5. Setting Short- and Long-Term Goals

Black and Hispanic students must be convinced that they can be what they *choose* to be in life. Teachers must help them understand that if they can "conceive it in their hearts and believe it, they can achieve it." As noted previously, these students also must be taught the importance of persistence.

In Table V, there is a "Success Chart" that can be used to help students set short- or long-range goals. This chart should be completed in the presence of the teacher. Students should first identify a goal they want to achieve by the age of 25. Next, students, with the help of the teacher, should list their outstanding qualities and those things that are likely to help them reach their goals. They also should develop specific strategies for achieving this long-term goal. Teachers can help by acknowledging student strengths and by letting the students know their intent is to help them reach their goal. Teachers also can indicate a willingness to help students overcome those weaknesses the students feel might be impeding their progress.

TABLE V
THE SUCCESS CHART

Student Name _____

Goal (Something you would like to have, become, or accomplish by the age of 25):

_____

_____

_____

_____

HELP:

List qualities or characteristics you possess that will help you reach *your goal:*

_____

_____

_____

HINDER:

List things that could possibly hurt or limit your efforts to reach *your goal:*

_____

_____

_____

Strategies for achieving this goal:

1. _____
2. _____
3. _____

NOTE: This same procedure can be used for short-range goals (e.g., Something you'd like to do within the next three weeks). For short-range goals, list specific steps to be taken and include a time frame.

Taken from Kuykendall, C. *Improving Black Student Achievement by Enhancing Student Self-Image*, Mid Atlantic Equity Center of American University, Washington, D.C. 1989.

In addition to the use of this success chart, teachers can:

- Schedule a monthly "show-and-tell" in which students share with the class non-school-related goals they have set and accopmlished.

- Have weekly reviews of famous Black and Hispanic Americans who have achieved their goals. Continue to remind students that success is very much a part of *their* culture and experience.

- Applaud all efforts students put forth to reach their goals.

- Set monthly academic achievement goals with and for each student and share them with parents or guardians.

- Assist students in developing sequential strategies for meeting goals.

- Help students to see failure as a learning experience by discussing failure as part of the road to success.

Students can also be inspired by the role model they see in their teachers, especially their Black and Hispanic teachers. Far too many teachers are discouraged because they believe their students lack adequate role models in their homes and communities. Rather than concern themselves with the influences outside of the school over which they have no control, teachers can make the most of the time they have with students. Remember, most students spend more time interacting with their "school family" (approximately six hours every day) than they spend interacting with their "home family." A teacher's exemplary behavior and aspirations can have a tremendous influence on students' drive and goal orientation. Finally, teachers and administrators must be willing to reward students who fulfill their goals. Students are motivated by rewards; and when success is rewarded, it is reinforced.

For example, Eastern High School in Washington, D.C., sponsors four "Student of the Month" awards. The winners, top students who have been recommended by teachers, get $15, a certificate, their pictures on a plaque in the school lobby, breakfast with a Kiwanis Club member, and lunch on Capitol Hill with the principal and a school board member. This program is designed to boost the image of students who are doing well, and to make success a cultural norm for the school.

Educators must work very hard to dispel the belief that it doesn't pay to do well academically. Children can be motivated to succeed through inspirational examples. As often as possible, teachers should allow students to discuss local success stories, such as:

- the experiences of city or county council representatives who might have lived in the students' neighborhood or attended their school and who set goals they reached.

- the accomplishments of elementary or high school alumni who also reached goals they set.

- the triumphs of local business persons or community leaders or family members who overcame setbacks.

- the experiences of local entertainers or sports heroes.

- the road to success taken by educators, including their own teachers.

- examine the lives of national heroes, past and present, especially those whose early lives were similar to the students'.

Keep students inspired and let them know victory can and will be theirs. They have to believe in their own abilities and the power within themselves in order to reach personal goals.

6. Develop Appropriate Teaching Styles

Many Black and Hispanic students respond favorably to extensive interaction with the teacher and other peers. I strongly encourage hugging, encouraging pats on the back, and other gestures that may involve touching in a supportive and nurturing manner, especially for younger children. The contact should be sincere and supportive, not intrusive. Teachers should also supplement the use of objects (i.e., computers and other learning devices) with person-to-person interaction, proximity, and lots of assurance. In addition, teachers should be sure to:

- speak in a comforting, consoling, but firm and determined voice.

- demonstrate fairness in the treatment of students.

- incorporate humor in their interaction with the class or individual students.

- develop rapport with students, and suggest that other test givers do the same, before administering an exam.

Maintain a high level of openness and acceptance with Black youth who engage in "stage setting." These are activities deemed important and necessary by some Black youth before engaging in an assignment (e.g., pencil sharpening, rearranging posture, checking paper and writing space, asking for repeat directions, and even checking perceptions with their neighbors). Many teachers are likely to perceive "stage setting" as an attempt to avoid work or disrupt class. However, this is an important activity for many Black youth.[10] Teachers can convey understanding and an acceptance of this need by allowing a few minutes for "stage setting" activities.

Demonstrate higher academic expectations. Teachers must not just tell students they believe in their abilities, they must *show* them. Convince these students that teachers believe in them and want them to excel by:

- using the classroom walls to display the work of all students in areas where they are skilled.

- writing encouraging notes on students' papers and to parents or guardians of elementary school students.

- maintaining a warm, inviting classroom climate through the use of appropriate attitudes and behaviors and bright and bold colors at all grade levels.

- encouraging students' natural exuberance, toning it down if necessary, without making students feel that they are wrong to show emotion.

- recognizing the knowledge and achievement of Black and Hispanic students in *all* areas.

Scheduling one-on-one sessions with students to discuss their weekly, monthly, and long-range goals is also helpful. Teachers can monitor progress and provide insight for ongoing improvement. If a heavy class load precludes meeting with each student, meet with a significant portion of students who require more attention.

Use a variety of other teaching strategies. Peer tutoring or coaching helps students on both sides. The phrase "each one teach one" should be a part of the class motto. Make good use of the "Buddy Game" which calls for pairing students who will be "buddy" to one another. Students spend time with their "buddies"—getting homework assignments in their absence, learning and sharing skills, information, and strategies. Encourage "buddies" to each make a list of all the strengths and talents that make their buddies special!

Have a "King" or "Queen" for a day where every child gets to play the part of "Class King" or "Class Queen." (Choose by lottery or alphabetically.) The King or Queen's buddy comes before the class and takes a few minutes to share everything *good* about his or her buddy. The teacher also shares good things about the honored student.

7) Use Homework and Television to Your Advantage

Homework should promote cooperation and communication among the teacher, the student, and the parent. It should help the child develop responsibility and independence, master a skill, and understand what has been taught. It should also encourage children to learn new things and keep parents informed about what their children are learning in school.[11]

Given the anticipated benefits of homework, teachers can make it a more powerful experience by:

- giving students homework projects that can involve members of their families; i.e., doing a family tree, assessing family strengths and virtues, writing fictional stories which feature family members as heroes/heroines, etc.

- giving students homework assignments which play to *their* strengths. A student athlete who has shown difficulty in reading might be asked to make an oral presentation on who might win the NBA Championship, Super Bowl or World Series after reviewing and analyzing newspaper stories on certain professional sports teams and developing his own logical conclusions.

- allowing students to watch television programs they normally watch, even though such programs may be considered negative. Students can write a paper on what makes such programs inappropriate and what negative values those programs impart.

- giving students assignments that require viewing more documentaries, educational programs, and programs dealing with current issues.

8) Communicate so that Your Real Intentions Are Understood

Cross-cultural miscommunication in the classroom does exist. Such miscommunication can lead to lower motivation and lower achievement, excessive speech/language therapy placements, perceptions of frequent, if unintentional, social insults from teachers and other students, frequent misunderstandings and misinterpretations from school personnel and other students, perception of negative school climate, and poor performance on tests and assessments.[12]

Teachers can avoid the consequences of cultural miscommunication through use of the following suggestions:

Become a more effective listener by keeping an open, curious mind; focus on the speaker's ideas while listening with feeling and intuition; become personally involved in what students say; ask for clarification when something is unclear; and listen to the essence of what's said.

Communication is conveyed from *total* person to *total* person. When we communicate, only 7% of what is conveyed comes from our words. 38% is non-verbal, through rate of speaking, tone and volume. 55% is non-vocal, through eye contact, body language, and posture.[13] Do not make the mistake of using negative body language; e.g., folded arms across the chest, inattentive eyes, clenched jaw, scowls, etc., when you're trying to send a positive message.

Help students to develop strong eye contact by having warm, encouraging eyes yourself. You may want to use an activity to strengthen eye contact. Allow students to work in small groups where they will cut out pairs of human eyes taken from magazines, articles, etc. Have them label what each set of eyes means; friendly eyes, fearless eyes, etc. Put some of these labeled eyes on a bulletin board. Students will be able to "look into eyes" throughout the day. This will become a habit-forming practice of looking into eyes. Believe me, it works!

9) Establishing a Good School and Classroom Climate

The climate of the classroom is the key to keeping students excited and motivated. There are climate variables that experts know affect behavior between students and teachers. The "climate" should not only welcome students but also keep them encouraged. In Chapter Six, more specific strategies are offered on creating a climate most conducive to achievement by Black and Hispanic students.

10) Strengthen Relations Between the Home and School

Most experts have concluded that the involvement of parents in the education of their children is essential to long-term school success.[14] However, many teachers do very little to encourage parental involvement and support. It should be emphasized that many parents simply do not know what they are "supposed" to be doing to enhance their child's academic self-image. Many have been socialized to believe that education is strictly the teacher's domain and that very little is required of them as parents. Teachers must reach out to parents and guardians and make them feel comfortable about the role they will play as equal partners in the education of their children. More specific strategies on strengthening this delicate bond will be shared in Chapter Seven.

These tips will work only if teachers *believe* they can make a difference. Half-hearted, lackluster implementation of any of these strategies will result only in failure. Even when these steps are followed enthusiastically, however, some teachers still may not meet with *immediate* success. All educators must remember that the same persistence we encourage in students *must* be used by school officials as well. Once these tips are put into practice, student discipline may be less problematic. The chapters that follow provide additional insight on creating the most conducive environment for good student behavior, student success, *and* teacher gratification.

Notes

1. Glasgow, D. *The Black Underclass: Poverty, Unemployment and Entrapment of Ghetto Youth.* San Francisco: Josset Bass Limited, 1980.

2. Fagan, J. and Jones, S.J. "Toward A Theoretical Model for Intervention with Violent Juvenile Offenders" in *Violent Youth Offenders,* Robert Mathias editor. San Francisco: National Council on Crime and Delinquency, CA 1984.

3. Kuykendall, C. *Improving Black Student Achievement by Enhancing Student Self-Image.* Washington, D.C.: Mid-Atlantic Equity Center, American University, 1989.

4. Howard, B. *Learning To Persist, Persisting To Learn.* Washington, D.C.: Mid-Atlantic Equality Center, 1987, American University.

5. Marks, W. *Strategies for Educational Change: Recognizing the Gifts and Talents of All Children.* New York: McMillan Publishing Co., 1981.

6. Fordham, S. and Ozbu, J. "Black Students' School Success: Coping with the Burden of Acting White." *The Urban Review,* Vol. 18, No. 3, 1986.

7. Beane, D. *Mathematics and Science: Critical Fillers for the Future of Minority Students.* Washington, D.C.: Mid-Atlantic Center for Race Equity, American University, 1988.

8. Howard, B. Op. Cit.

9. Fordham, S. and Ozbu, J. Op. Cit.

10. Gilbert, S. and Gay, G. "Improving The Success In School of Poor Black Children." *Phi Delta Kappen,* October 1985.

11. Kuykendall, C. *You and Yours: Making The Most of This School Year*, Washington, D.C.: Mid-Atlantic Equity Center of American University, 1987.

12. Taylor, Orlando, *Cross-Cultural Communication: An Essential Dimension of Effective Education.* Washington, D.C.: Mid-Atlantic Equality Center of American University, 1987.

13. Weinberg, G. and Catero. H. *How to Read A Person Like A Book*, New York: Hawthorn Books, 1971.

14. Henderson, A., "The Evidence Continues to Grow: Parent Involvement Improves Student Achievement," Columbia, MD: NCCE, 1987.

5 ADDRESSING THE NEED FOR DISCIPLINE

As the twig is bent, so the tree is inclined...

Anonymous

There is a need for effective classroom management. There is also a commensurate need to help students overcome obstacles to self-control and good self-discipline. While "good behavior" is necessary for all students to realize achievement gains, teachers have a better chance of increasing achievement motivation when they can develop in students the sense of responsibility, self-control, and the desire to achieve lifelong success.

The two basic causes of poor student behavior are internal—within the schools—and external—through family, peers, cultural influences, and other factors outside of the school.

Internal Causes of Poor Student Discipline

If a student feels unwelcome or like an intruder, that student may demonstrate the need to be an integral part of the class through disruptive behavior. This desire for inclusion calls attention to the dominant need of the student for recognition.

Quite often, disruptive students are responding to what *they* perceive as the teacher's belief in the student's inferiority. In such cases, students are likely to react with negative behavior that actually puts them in control of what happens in class. Similarly, some students satisfy their need for recognition, acceptance, appreciation, and inclusion by engaging in behavior that appears to be courting the rejection of the classroom teacher. Teachers should understand that many of these "hostile" and disruptive youth actually fear emotional slights from teachers. They may put up a hypersensitive defensive front to protect their feelings and emotions.

While it is true that some disruptive Black and Hispanic students are simply bored or restless, many are responding to or ventilating the rage they feel as a result of their loss of hope and their likely school failure. When schools fail to prepare youth for lifelong success, they are inviting trouble. A truly "hopeless" child is likely to be a real "problem" child as well. To augment the hope Black and Hispanic students need, teachers and schools must avoid institutional policies and programs such as tracking or ability grouping, which send signals of inferiority. Students are commonly placed in special education classes when it is the students' behavior rather than their ability that causes problems. This practice must be avoided if we are to help these students.

Many students are also likely to respond negatively to what they may perceive as unequal or unfair treatment. Selective rule enforcement, where some students are disciplined and other students are "excused" for committing the same infraction must be eradicated altogether.

The self-fulfilling prophecy about behavior still holds true in our schools. It is important that teachers don't communicate preconceived notions about behavioral tendencies or suggest that students are "bad," "uncouth," or more likely to misbehave than other students. If they do, the students are likely to behave accordingly.

The failure to provide students with frequent opportunities for success and accomplishment in the classroom is another contributing factor to poor behavior. Black and Hispanic students have a need to show what they can do, just as other students take pride in showing their work. If students are not given frequent opportunities for success through classroom activities, they are likely to satisfy the need for accomplishment by telling jokes or disrupting class.

External Causes of Poor Student Discipline

External causes of poor student discipline are rooted in family and cultural influences and the negative influence of peers.

While most teachers expect that parents will play a major role in disciplining their child, there are some parents who are unable to instill the values or develop the character requisite for appropriate school behavior. Some of these parents even have "given up" on their own children. Does this mean the schools should give up, too?

Some families actually reward children—or give tacit approval—to behavior that the school might find unacceptable. For example, some youth may come from homes where parents encourage speaking out, telling jokes, questioning rules, fighting back, or laughing out loud. In such instances, we cannot blame children for their lack of awareness of the cultural and communication norms which are valued by our educational institutions. We must help them to understand and appreciate appropriate behavioral norms without giving the impression that we are demanding "conformity" or that we dislike them because of their behavior. In addition, "parent awareness" conferences can take place between school officials and parents to make certain parents understand acceptable and unacceptable behavior.

Peer groups obviously play a big role in mitigating or enhancing behavioral problems. As noted previously, many youth develop an "us versus them" mentality when they think the school has already rejected them. These students feel that the only support they have comes from peers who see teachers as "the enemy." Schools must break down this alienation or discipline problems will continue. Teachers can influence students and their rebellious peer groups through strategies de-

signed to reflect genuine concern, support, and some under-
standing.

Strategies for Discipline Problems

There have been numerous suggestions throughout this
book for enhancing student self-image and motivation. How-
ever, there are many other things teachers can do. Teachers
must first check their own attitudes and motivations, incorpo-
rate classroom strategies with the greatest likelihood of reduc-
ing discipline problems, and use appropriate activities and
strategies once poor behavior surfaces.

Checking Your Attitude. While it may be hard to be-
lieve, there are actually some teachers who *don't like* certain
children. This dislike comes across not only to that student,
but to other students as well. Teachers who find it difficult to
like a particular child should seek instead to love the "human-
ity" in that child. If the teacher cannot "love" the child's hu-
manity, that teacher should question whether or not he or she
belongs in this profession.

Marva Collins suggests telling some poorly disciplined
children—on a daily basis—what you like about them and
seeking to discern what they like about themselves.[1] When
students know there is a bond of genuine admiration and
appreciation, they are more receptive to suggestions from the
teacher regarding behavior which might be changed. Once
adequate bonding has occurred, teachers can get students to
discuss behavior they would like to change or improve in
themselves.

Teachers also should develop the attitudes that *there are
no "bad children,"* just *"inappropriate behavior."* I recall that
when I was a young and sometimes quite mischievous child,
my mother would remind me of her intense love for me, even
when she was acknowledging her strong dislike for inappro-
priate behavior. I continued to do this as a parent and teacher.

Teachers will be unable to implement strategies and activities which will prevent student misbehavior if they believe:

- most Black and Hispanic youth are just "bad kids."

- a "good" student is a "quiet" student.

- a "good" class is a class where there is no active learning, no movement, or student interaction.

- students learn best when there is no class noise.

- children are being disrespectful when they challenge a teacher's fairness.

- all youth who crack jokes, laugh loudly, or show nonconformity in dress, personal appearance, or dialect are inherently underachievers.

Using "Preventive Strategies". Once students get the message that *their* education and lifelong success is the *school's* priority, they are more likely to respond with favorable and positive behavior. This message is conveyed through the effective use of teaching styles that have a positive impact on student motivation. As they exist now, many schools and classrooms are not structured to facilitate the achievement of many Black and Hispanic students. Classrooms are still predominantly "teacher centered" as opposed to "student centered." Many teachers still engage in behavior which suggests they are impersonal, aloof, and uncomfortable with the existence of diverse populations in their schools. Even in some all-Black schools, some Black teachers have been known to behave towards some of their lower-class students in ways that suggest the student is not wanted. As indicated previously, student reaction to perceived indifference is predictably negative.

The following additional suggestions will help teachers to deter students from becoming discipline problems:

Make certain you have taken time with the student to discuss *one-on-one* the student's lifelong goals and how the experience in *your* class will help facilitate fulfillment of that lifelong goal. If you have not already used the "Success Chart" presented in Table V, plan to do so immediately with a student who is prone to "acting up."

Plan to build on the non-academic strengths of every student. If a student is overly aggressive, make him a class "leader." Give him or her some kind of responsibility for maintaining and generating the cooperation of other students in class activities. If you have a real "clown" on your hands, give him a daily assignment to start or end the class with a humorous act that will also share a *positive* message. Remember, all children have a special gift or talent. Creative and effective teachers are able to augment student motivation by providing opportunities for each of these "gifted" students to shine. In so doing, these teachers are able to offset the negative actions of children who are seeking recognition in the class.

Provide opportunities for success and accomplishment. Black and Hispanic students are more likely to engage in non-conformist, deviant classroom behavior when they are not given opportunities to succeed at *something*. Teachers should assign class projects for potentially disruptive youth that not only build on that child's individual and cultural strengths but which will satisfy the need for success. For example, students can be asked to complete an assignment that calls for them to describe their own experiences and contrast them with the experiences of other students. Students might also be given an assignment which calls for them to respond to open-ended questions, such as "what do you think would have happened if...." Such an activity will not only provide an opportunity for successful completion, it also will enhance the critical-thinking skills of the student.

Enhance responsibility by giving students a role to play in maintaining a "manageable" classroom. Many students are unmotivated and disruptive because of teacher behavior that stresses adult domination and student obedience.[2] According to research by McClelland, adult domination occurs when adults prescribe what a youth is to do and how it is to be done.

McClelland also concluded that adults who stress obedience and conformity in order to develop "polite and manageable" children inadvertently lower achievement motivation.[3]

Teachers can enhance the clarification of positive values and improve responsible behavior in Black and Hispanic students by making them a part of the rule-enforcement process. Teachers can divide students into small work groups and give each group the task of determining, *as a group*, ten rules that should govern all classroom behavior. Each group also must agree on appropriate consequences for rule violations. Each small group then presents to the whole class the rules and consequences they developed. It would be helpful if students were provided with newsprint and markers to record their decisions.

Once every group has presented its consensus determination on appropriate rules and the reasons *why* they felt these rules should be enforced, the class votes on the rules and consequences by which they will be governed. One complete list of rules and consequences is then placed in a prominent place in the classroom for everyone to see.

This activity will improve student behavior by giving them a feeling of "ownership" for the structure and operation of the classroom. More importantly, this activity also will enhance the students' sense of responsibility, their acceptance of positive values and behavioral norms, and the cohesion among students in the classroom. Children are more likely to support and encourage other children when they share responsibility, purpose, and common values.

Show students your respect for them individually and collectively. Some teachers resort to behavior that belittles, demeans, and destroys student bonding and self-confidence when they are confronted with inappropriate student behavior. The disrespect of these teachers for their students is demonstrated through unnecessarily harsh tones, a denial of student requests for assistance, nonverbal body language, superior attitudes, and unequal enforcement of rules. In most children's programs, it does not take long to see that adults expect to be treated with more respect than they demonstrate.[4]

Establish trusting relationships with students. Marva Collins suggests making friends with students, complimenting them, letting them know how much they were missed when they have been absent, and even sitting with them during lunch.[5] Teachers also can take time to discuss with students any real or perceived problems that student may be having at home, in the school (with other teachers or students), or in other environments.

What to Do When They Still Misbehave

Even when a teacher feels he has been supportive, respectful, and caring, students may still behave "inappropriately." Teachers should understand that many Black and Hispanic youth often are socialized with attitudes and strategies designed to enhance their survival in a White environment that is more often than not perceived to be hostile. These students are taught to appreciate some skills and behavioral norms that are not always condoned in our classrooms. Some of those skills that may be prized in their respective communities, but not in our schools, include nonverbal communication, dance and rhythmic movements, rapping, learning through cooperative dependence on others, and verbal interplay during instruction.

Teachers must still socialize Black and Hispanic students to live both inside and outside of their own cultural groups. However, teachers risk further alienation when they refuse to understand or appreciate the cultural values, norms, and communication patterns these youth bring to the learning environment.

Even when students behave inappropriately, teachers may be able to use adverse behavior as an opportunity to facilitate student growth and acceptance of corrective behavioral norms. The following tips should help:

Punish the Behavior—Not the Person. It is important that this distinction be made. Teachers must inform students constantly—through spoken and written reminders and supportive behavior—that they respect and admire them as individuals. Once students understand that the consequences are for inappropriate behavior rather than the students' existence, they are more likely to modify the behavior and to accept the guidance of well-meaning adults.

Discipline Students with a Firm but "Loving Touch." If there is no love, no genuine concern, no desire to help, the disciplinary act is likely to lead to bitterness and resentment, not maturity.[6] Renowned educator Marva Collins offers the following guideposts for dealing with disruptive students:[7]

- Have students write compositions or deliver three-minute speeches on the etymology of gum, rather than punitive lines such as, "I will not chew gum in class."

- Continue to reward and compliment them for good behavior and take extra teaching time, either before or after school, to help students who are slower and more likely to misbehave.

Use Creative Alternatives to Suspension, Detention and Isolation. Many school districts use alternative suspension programs, or "in-school" suspension. Quite often, however, even these well-meaning alternatives defeat their purpose. In many in-school suspension programs, students simply go to a room with other "disruptive" students and a "caretaker" adult where they are allowed to do everything *other than learn* from their behavior.

In such "alternative suspension" programs, students should be asked to prepare papers on the impact of their behavior on other students, how their behavior has detracted from their pursuit of legitimate lifelong goals, or how a modification of behavior might make them better people. Most importantly, students should be disciplined in such a way that they do not distance themselves totally from the learning process.

Many times, students who exhibit inappropriate behavior are retained, put out of the class, or put into special education classes. Unless they are given opportunities to assess the impact of their behavior and to analyze reasons for behavioral change, such practices will do more harm than good.

Teachers will always be faced with mischievous and disruptive students. Even when students display a mischievous streak, however, they still deserve opportunities for transformation and academic growth. A good teacher can make certain such opportunities are always a part of the school day.

Finally, teachers must make effective use of climate variables that affect student behavior and student attitudes toward self. These climate variables, and the need for an environment that is more conducive to learning and more encouraging school buildings, are discussed in the next chapter.

Notes

1. Collins, M. *Marva Collins' Way*. Los Angles: Jeremy P. Tarcher, Inc., 1990.

2. McClelland, D. "Sources of An Achievement" in McClelland, D. and Stelle, R. (editors) *Human Motivation*. Morristown, NJ: General Learning Press, 1973. Taken from Brendtro, L., Brokenleg, M. and Van Dochern, S. *Reclaiming Youth at Risk*. Bloomington, IN: National Educational Service, 1990.

3. Ibid.

4. Brendtro, L., Brokenleg, M. and Van Bochern, S. *Reclaiming Youth At-Risk*. Bloomington, IN: National Educational Service, 1990.

5. Collins, M. op. cit.

6. Ibid.

7. Ibid.